VETERANS BENEFITS

Tim Connelly

Copyright@2007 by Tim Connelly

All rights reserved. No part of this book may be reproduced in any manner without written consent except for the quotation of short passages used inside of an article, criticism. or review.

ISBN 978-0-6151-7018-3

We entered grade school
not as friends
just classmates.
Bugsey,
tall, skinny, thick, black framed glasses
always gave me crap for being overweight.
He left school in junior high
and ended up going to war.
Dick
 slicked back black hair and cowboy boots
was always picking on kids.
put a mouse in his mouth
to scare the girls.
Dick left school in 11th grade
and ended up going to war.
Ernie
from the farm
smelled like manure.
always talked about sex.
We made fun of him.
He quit school in eight grade
ended up going to war.
Tony

and I were altar boys.
We would sneak some communion wine
Sister Odeil would give us a hard time.
Tony left school his senior year
ended up going to war.
Roger was just a face in the crowd.
no one remembers Roger leaving school
but he too
ended up going to war.

Bugsey
drives a cab at night
and lives in a one room apartment.
He has his share of drinking bouts
and urinates on the bathroom floor
then wonders why it stinks.
Dick
won many medals in the war.
He works at night cleaning buildings.
They say he did some prison time.

Ernie
went to war twice
and came back to the farm.

He started drinking
 and raising hell
and shot himself one day
while in the barn.
Tony
sits in his room all day
and smokes cigarettes,
drinks beer and
watches porno movies.
The voices in his head
telling him he is soon to be dead.
Roger
came home from war
just another body in a box.
I
ended up going to war
then drank to much
and nearly lost my mind
but never hope.

One day
I fell in love with a woman.
She taught me to love myself
and put the memories

of shattered lives
to rest.

War persists in the mind
through a lifetime.
As a person looks back
they ask what happened
who was I
who did I become?
To understand the changes
that war has made in a man
requires the passage of time
and distance from the way
he remembers himself.
Some who have gone to war,
have a deep need to record
what they saw and felt,
to find meaning
to find themselves.

I have a recurring dream
of being in a field,
surrounded by bodies
laid side by side.
The air smells.
My job
is to get the names,
ages, and hometowns
of the dying victims.
I never get past
the fifth victim
before I get sick.
Someone tells me
to go home.
I beg to stay
and that's when
I wake up horrified.
I never know

if I am horrified
by the field full of death
or my inability
to get the job done.
All the details of death
and disaster have accumulated
inside me.
At times I delighted
in the absurdity of the days events.
I told jokes,
products of gallows humor,
to save my sanity.
I believed,
at one time,
I made a difference
and that people cared.
I miss the jolts of adrenaline.
I miss the talented
and purposeful people
that worked with me.
I miss the wholesome insanity
and unhealthy pace.
Part of me still remains
in that crowded,
noisy, airless,

and windowless building.

The doctor continues
with his dire predictions.
I will be unable
to resolve my depression
in less than a month.
It's going to take some time.
The doctor thinks I'm
in to good a mood,
after just being fired
from my job.
He says my job loss
is a chance to start over
and do something
I really wanted to do.
I don't want to reframe anything.
I going to be humiliated
by the family for being out of work.

Of course, it's my choice
to offer myself as a doormat.
"You might have to continue
being a doormat for awhile," the doctor says.
as he continues
with his pessimistic approach.
Because encouraging me
to do better
might serve a paradoxical end.
I get out of bed
late most days.
I go downtown
and buy some newspapers,
talk with a few people,
and then ride the bus.
At home,
I read the papers,
eat and watch TV.
into the late night.
Day after day.
I have to break the routine
soon but I like
my isolated life style.
It's comfortable and safe.
I also feel a lot of shame

because I'm overweight,
I tip the scales
at more than 300 pounds.
The doctor says
my sense of futility
is related
to a deep sense of shame
about my weight
and rejection in my family.

Doctors Note:

What has emerged
is a picture of a man
who has moved
very slowly
through career opportunities
inspite of his talents
and abilities.
It is almost
as though
he were moving slowly
so as to consolidate
his ground
because of his own

personal lack
of sense of security.
He tends
to use his creativity
more in service
to other people
by producing for them
than he does
investing for himself.
If he did move
with his creativity
he could possibly
move more quickly
than he is able
to feel comfortable with.

I'm frustrated
and angry.
I'm not able to do more.
It's hard
to label my feelings
and that contributes to my confusion.
The origins of my shame
are focused around my family
and failed jobs.

I'm maintaining
a passive approach to therapy.
I believe
it should be a process
in which the doctor and myself
work together
to discover the barriers
to my living life,
the way I want to.
"It's like a jigsaw puzzle,
the picture of which is not known beforehand,"
the doctor preaches.
The description
appeals to my intellectual curiosity
and seems non-threatening.
I do have choices in my life.
The plan is to continue
at a slow pace
and focus on feelings
rather than a specific behavior change.

I expect to be rejected by people
because I don't like myself.
I can't meet my own standards.
I was more content in the Army

during the war.
I was in charge of things
and not questioned,
accepted as a competent person.
It was the case too
when I was a one man newsroom
for a radio station.
I'm reluctant to follow up
on any radio work.
I'm inferior
and see no point
in pretending I can
be employed or successful.
The feelings of being inadequate
and incompetent socially
goes back many years.
I have times when I
feel more comfortable about my abilities
and less inferior.
It's clear,
however,
no one can logically convince me
that I'm not inferior.
The belief is serving
some function

such as an excuse
to help me avoid
dealing with the specter of failure.

I have difficulty
accepting the respect of others.
I don't even like
or respect myself.
The doctor says
my early childhood
is related to my failure
to establish
self esteem and self respect.
Apparently something to do
with my father's drinking problem.
I spent a lot of time
with my mother and grandmother as a kid.
I always wished my father
was like the fathers of my friends.
I don't like sharing that fact.
I'm still interested in therapy
but have little optimism
how it can change the future.
I expect to be rejected by others
and eventually fail.

Why look for a catalyst for change?

I'm a candidate for a job
but didn't do will in the interview.
I'm not enthusiastic.
I'm unwilling
to take even the smallest risks
or even challenge my assumptions
about what other people think of me.
I'm spending more hours each day
in front of the TV
and my energy level
is running on batteries.
It's not comfortable
sitting around all day watching television
but it feels like a better alternative
than exploring the different possibilities in my life.
It's not clear
what I'm accomplishing by seeing a shrink.
It's my only real contact
with another human being
as most of my relationships are quite superficial.
The doctor's becoming frustrated
with my passive approach to therapy.
I'm just not ready

or willing to accept responsibility
for changing the way I do things.

My mind's a blank.
I've nothing to say to the doctor.
I don't want to talk about myself
or my memories of childhood.
I never had goals,
just a typical adolescent
who wasn't interested in going to college.
My big thrill
was going to keg parties in the woods
with my friends
and drinking beer and smoking cigars.
After high school,
I worked as a hospital orderly
and lived with a buddy
until I joined the Army,
My mother was a typical housewife
who worked part-time,
while my father worked
in a local grocery store.
I saw my father
as a low inertia person
who I'm probably most like.

I was expected to move to the city,
get a job at one of the big employers
and that would be it.
Translated into a personal philosophy:
"Life is tough, and then you die."
I tend to keep people at an emotional distance
with my wit and flare for the dramatic presentation.
The doctor wants to hypnotize me,
and thinks I'm abusing alcohol
even though an earlier consultation
makes it obvious I'm not chemically dependent.

The MMPI

The test placed me in the high average range of intelligence
and suggests an acutely depressed and anxious man with
feelings of despondency and pessimism and suicidal
ruminations. I am fearful of nearly everything and am
constantly worried and guilt-ridden. I'm vulnerable to minimal
threat and overreact to minor matters. I'm fearful of emotional
dependency and of emotional involvement. I show obsessive
features and perfectionism and see myself as a failure and am

very self critical and intropunitive. I'm apathetic, weak, tired, fatigued, unable to concentrate well and ambivalent about making decisions. I'm troubled by my sexual feelings, and have a lot of sexual conflicts, and show sexual role confusion. Also the scores are significant for alcoholism.

My expectations
of therapy are very mixed.
I'm both impatient for results
yet expect practically nothing to happen.
Being fired from the radio station
was the start of my current feelings of failure.
I sued the radio station.

What's most damaging
is what people say in their depositions.
My boss accuses me of doing nothing,
of only reading newspapers
while I was supposed to be working.
A coworker says
I was "as colorful as a door knob."
The accusations hurt
and I have questioned myself
about my effectiveness
as a person ever since.
I've no ability
to see my own resources.
I'm fragile and apprehensive
whenever I talk about my self-perspective.
I've difficulty
following through with plans.
I can't set any specific goals
because I feet embarrassed, empty and afraid.
If I'm ever going to change
I'm going to face rejection and failure.

I'm fed up.
My doctor's perplexed
but wants to continue support

but doesn't want to push me
into any specific action.
It seems the best way
to deal with a person
who shows fear of rejection
and animosity towards authority figures.
I'm hopeless and demoralized
that life happens
while you're planning for it.
I'm committed to no action
to get myself out of my current rut.
I'm going to end up on welfare
and
I don't want to consider an alternative route.
I'm caught up in my own ambivalence
of not wanting to be told what to do
but not knowing what to do
when left to my own devices.
All things considered,
I'm essentially
in the same existential dilemma
which has been bothering me for years.

Commentary

Existentialists are very much concerned about the human situation and point to the breakdown of traditional values, the depersonalization of human beings in society and the loss of meaning in human existence. Trying to shape one's own identify, finding satisfying values, and living a constructive and meaningful life are more difficult than ever before. Existential neurosis is a person's inability to succeed in that quest. In fact, most people after "taking stock" are confronted with the sickening realization that their busy and seemingly important lives have really not proven meaningful or fulfilling.

One Year Later
Doctor's Note

He has returned to the clinic again
with his vague complaints.
The event this time
involves a change in management at his job.
The boss is an "idiot" according to him.
What this tends to do to him
is make him feel less worthwhile,
less able to function properly,
and less likely to be assertive
and utilize what he already knows and has.
It's nearly impossible
to get from him
what specifically he's looking for
by coming to the clinic.
He knows that it's a crisis for him
because he's debating
whether or not to leave his job
and has no specific therapeutic goal.
He has no one outside of work to talk with
and needs a place for supportive communication.

I'm visibly shaken
while my sister proceeds to talk anxiously.

I apparently didn't invent emotional cut off in my family,
yet I may have perfected it.
My sister rationalizes reasons
she keeps her distance from the family by working.
She speaks with tenderness and affection
about her older brother.
Our mother's death has intensified the family cut off.
I'm tearful
and initially
unable to identify
what I'm feeling
yet knowing,
however,
that all my usual ways of avoiding feelings
are not working.

My father
wonders if there is anything

he can do to help me.
It was a big shock
when I entered the Army.
The family didn't expect me to enlist.
When I wrote home from basic training
all I was told to do was kill, kill, kill, kill...
When I came home from the war
I seemed in pretty good shape
but stayed at home and drank.
My father had done the same thing
after World War II.
My father minimizes his four years
in the South Pacific with the Marines
and tries more or less to forget about it.
He doesn't have any nightmares
but certain dates are bad...
like Christmas.
When my father was a kid on the farm
he never thought of war
and was totally unprepared.
We used to get together
but I have never been back home
since my mother died a few
years ago.

I attend a session about the family
with some other men.
I sit quietly and listen attentively
and don't miss one word.
I predictably
interjected some emotionally
impactful statement
which is always extremely accurate
and indicative of my insight
and ability to pull things together
and point it out in such a way
that the other men understand.
I talk about being rocketed once in awhile
and having no bunker in which to escape
and therefore had to remain
with the sick and wounded
while the enemy fire continued.
I put patients under the bed
and those that were not able to move
were covered with mattresses.
I wasn't issued a weapon
so I was even more vulnerable
and unable to defend myself.

I'm afraid to go to sleep
or take my night medication.
I wake up in my sitting room chair
in the middle of the night
without recalling how I've gotten there.
It makes me wonder
if something is going wrong.
I don't have an appointment with the doctor
for another month.
I'm afraid that I will wake-up
 some place I don't want to be.

The Group
October 31
Week One

I sit in a sparsely decorated room
at the Post Trauma Stress Clinic
with three other men.
It'll be a seven week process
trying to deal with events of a war,
which has left nightmares, flashbacks,
anger and depression.
It gets worse before it gets better
I'm told.
It's Halloween.
A good day to dig up the ghosts
which have been haunting us.
I came to Minneapolis many years ago
to begin the journey off to war
now perhaps this trip to Minneapolis
would begin the journey home.

Dr. Harry Russell
the program psychologist.

introduces the program.
I'm still not sure about him.
Dr. Edwin Smelker is the psychiatrist.
He's funny but
I feel resentment towards him.
because he is a W.W.II veteran.
Clay King is the social worker.
He bugs me.
Jean Miller is the occupational therapist.
She is nice and is also my coordinator.
Kay Ryan is the nurse.
She talks about family issues.
The patients are Dave the engineer
who is also suicidal.
He was a recon man in the war.
He is having marital problems
and talks too much.
My first impression
I don't like the guy.

David is heavily drugged
or something and says very little.
He was in the airborne.
Mike was a medic.
He is nervous

and makes me nervous.

Art was a grunt.

He's a biker.

He is the strong silent type.

Then, there is me.

After a short break,

some guy talks to us about benefits,

education, employment and so forth.

He will be seeing us again individually.

At noon we get a bag lunch

with mystery meat sandwiches.

We sit around and listen

as Dave talks nonstop about the war.

About 1pm

we go to occupational therapy.

We cut out pictures from old magazines

to show how we feel about our life

and goals at the current time.

David hates the exercise and doesn't take part.

We wrap up around 2:30 for the first day.

I don't know if this program

will help a thing.

I will try it out for awhile.

Tuesday:

We see a film
about a stress program in California.
We also have a new group member.
Dan was a medic in the Navy
and was attached to the Marines.
His whining voice drives me up the wall.
At the end of the movie,
Dave and Dan start crying.
Mike and myself are uneasy
with this display of emotion
and walk out of the room.
About 10 we start talking
about our war experiences in group.
Dave is the most vocal.
He suffers from guilt
over the deaths of two squad members
and for some reason wants to go
into the woods and kill people.
Dave and Mike are at odds
with some type of personality conflict.
Later in OT we draw a life line.
Mike seems to have a lot of personal problems
with his wife, home, kids and job.
Dan seems to be screwed up with his family life too.

Friday:

I have lost a couple of days.
I was going to be faithful
to this journal
I'm being half assed as usual.
I'm overwhelmed and
my memory is jammed.
What happened yesterday?
I can't really remember.
I wonder if I'm aware
of my guilt feelings
about the war.
Is it guilt of who I was,
rather than what I did or didn't do?
Am I in touch with the meaning
events had on me?
Is it guilt over my curiosity
in the face of death
and the sense I had been an onlooker?
Do I need to confess?
Is the guilt an outgrowth of fear?
Or does guilt increase fear.
Is it guilt over having suffered

less than others?
I was an onlooker in war
I'm still doing it to this day.
I stand back from involvement.
I want to become less of an onlooker in life
but am afraid I will break down like during the war.
There's stress involving experiences
with sick, wounded, dying, and
dead soldiers and civilians.
I think I was proficient at times.

Tuesday:
In group we discuss
what I did in the war.
I can't read a story
about my experiences
I do show some pictures
I'm angry but didn't know why.
I tremble
as I slap my leg
with my hand,
tears roll down my cheeks.
"Hey man why do you feel guilty

when you were trying to save people,"
Art asks, "while I was trying to kill people.
I'm the one with guilt."
Mike had been a medic.
and was wounded in a firelight
and pinned down for eight hours.
He couldn't move
after being hit by a grenade.
It had been so surreal a feeling to him.
He was a medic
and couldn't do anything
for the guys being shot-up
all around him.
David screams,
"For all anyone cares
we might as well all be dead."
Why did I get myself into this shit.
In OT we paint pictures.
Mine looks at war from a distance.
A drawing of a face
one half light the other dark.
I'm upset.
Damn, I don't understand why.

Week Three
Monday:

I'm extremely nervous.
I didn't want to come today.
I'm staying at a place
called Heilman House
a place for homeless veterans.
Six guys to a room.
It reminds me of the barracks in Germany.
Old, dark and hot.
I don't want to stay here.
Art didn't show today.
I don't think he will come back.
Heilman House or Hell House sucks.
 Why

did I get myself into this shit.
I just want to be happy.

Tuesday:

David talks about an officer
who died in an ambush.
David cared for the guy
and is angry about how
the man's body was treated
with no respect.
The body was dragged in the mud.
David also says a friend named Willie
was killed, his body stripped and castrated.
He still has a recurring nightmare about the incident.
It's the first time David has really opened up.
He feels exhausted.
I think we all do.
Mike is jumpy today.

He needs a job
his problem with his wife
is not getting better.
Art didn't show again today.
I am not focused.
I hate Hell House
and worry about money.
I don't know if this program
is really worth it.

Wednesday:

First snow storm of the season.
Art is missing for a third day.
I'm depressed.
David says he was in a porn movie
at age 16 after he ran away from home to LA.
I sit silent in the corner.
I don't see any therapeutic value in this bullshit.
We draw pictures about our view of ourselves.
Mine is negative as usual.
I want to go home.

Thursday:
Art returned after being sick

with a cold for a few days.
Dan says we owe our enemies
an apology.
There is going to be a lot of down time today
for some reason.
Mike seems in a better mood
Dave hasn't talked much all this week.
I feel tense.
Back at Hell House with the boys on the edge.
Damn, if this place doesn't motivate me,
I don't know what will.

Friday:

Art didn't show today.
Dr. Smelker leads group.
Mike seems in better spirits.
David seems spaced out.
Dave is laid back.
I feel like a bundle of depressed nerves.
Dan has finally stopped his whining episodes.

Week Four:

David is late today

Mike is stuck in traffic
everyone seems in a good mood.
Dave is more distant and withdrawn.
Dan says he is scared
but is getting more into things.
I don't know what I feel.
I am a professional depressant.
I am on welfare with no hope in sight.
I need a job and hate living in Hell House.
I don't think anyone understands
where I am coming from anymore.
Jean wants me to contact my family
or call one of the other guys in the program
or to get in touch with an old high school buddy
I just don't want to bother people.
Jean is pushing me to get out and see the city.
I hate the city.
I want to be off in some small town
stuck in an apartment.
It's a safe rut to be in
and comfortable.
It would be my choice
not someone elses.
Other people don't know
what is best for me.

Besides the city is enemy territory
I don't venture out in an unsecured area
without backup
or self protection-like the handgun
I keep in my backpack.

Tuesday:

Art talks about a friend
who was killed
and how he always wanted
to go see the parents of the man
and tell them how their son died.
He now feels he has the nerve to do it.
Dr. Smelker says talking with the parents
will give the death of Art's friend
some sense of meaning.
Art talks about being a funeral color guard
for a man from his home town.
He had a tough time dealing
with the experience and
says the mother of the dead soldier
refused to accept the American flag.
Art seems to be opening up
while I close down.

I can't relate to these guys.
Dave gets kind of emotional.
I sense a lot of bitter feelings
in that man.
He is scary.
Mike is hyper
I don't know what is eating him
he doesn't know either.
Dan begins whining again
when he tells a story
it just drives me nuts.
David is spaced out as usual.
He says JFK's death
really means something to him now
before it didn't mean a thing.
It hit home like a rocket, he says.
I am uncomfortable
sick of talking and listening
to stories about the war.
Mike asks if I feel guilt
over not being in a combat unit.
Maybe? Of course.
We make masks.
Mine is the Lone Ranger.
Mike is good at art

his mask looks professional.
Dan has a lump of something for a mask.
Dave has a black faced death mask.
David and Art are not really into the project…
in their words "it's a lot of bullshit."

Wednesday:

I'm nervous.
I dread going to group.
I'm prepared to read
some stuff I have written
while killing time at Hell House.
Kay Ryan talks about social isolation.
I know a lot about the subject.
I don't offer any feedback

she says I'm a hard case.
Mike went to get medical assistance
for his wife and missed group.
We talk about the jobs we have held
 and the relationship of the war
and the ability to stay employed.
David tells about his many jobs.
His biggest fear about work
is relating well with other people
Once he was a bus driver for the city.
He got upset one day
with the people on the bus.
So he parked the vehicle
and walked away from the job
leaving the passengers stranded.
We all have a common thread
dealing with other people
and the anger and anxiety it causes
with work.
We continue mask making.
We will have four days of freedom
because of the Thanksgiving holiday.
I'm thankful to get out of here.

Week Five
Monday:

I feel guilty.
I should be out in the mainstream
as a productive, functioning person
in the real work world.
I should be looking for a job

to pay my bills.
I can't afford
to pay anything to anyone.
I don't know what to do.
I will apply for social services.
I need some advice.
Dr. Smelker says I am rather boring.
We get a lecture on guilt and shame.
The guilt has to do with the fact
we feel good for not getting killed, others did.
Mike expresses feelings of not doing enough.
Shame.
I'm not any good
I never was.
I'm confused on the guilt issue.
I'm not sure if or what
I 'm guilty about.
Is it survivor guilt?
I have a cold
and feel uncomfortable
and overwhelmed by everything.
Jean says I appear to be sadder
but more calm and not as nervous.
She says it looks as if I could cry.
That's exactly how I do feel.

I let a few tears out
as I discuss how lonely I feel.
Jean wants me to express those feelings
in group and ask for help
in being less isolated.
I don't know.
We draw pictures about how we feel
and see ourselves as group members.
Dan draws the spokes of a wheel.
He is really out of it and down on himself.
I draw a goofy picture of a flower,
balloons and bugs.
Art draws six guys in a boat, adrift.
 David draws different types of faces
while Mike draws us
as pieces of a puzzle
Dave draws a pair of dice.
We represent the six black spots.
Dan says he doesn't belong in group,
and doesn't think the war
is the root of his problems.
Dr. Smelker wants to hear more from me.
Dave and Mike seem more upbeat.
I still feel like shit .
Another evening at Hell House.

Tuesday:

It's 6 am.
I sit here in Hell House
I want to leave.
This is the strongest urge yet to run.
David is very silent today.
Dave is not very talkative
and is very cool and non- feeling
when he does say something.
He talks about the war
and can't remember the names
of friends killed in action.
Mike says he is proud
of winning the bronze star
and purple heart
but nobody really cares
or cared after he returned home.
He worked at his peak
during the war
and figured
he was going to die anyway.
He had a spiritual experience
but can't reason why

he has trouble working
at that peak effort now days
or if he ever can again.
Mike has a recurring dream
about dying.
Art says he has a similar dream
of being shot
and tells of being ambushed
and how an enemy soldier
pointed a gun at him
but it didn't fire.
There was no bullet
in the chamber.
He took a shot
at the enemy the next day
but he didn't know
if it was the same guy.
He feels guilty
about the whole incident.
Art says the PTSD program
won't make any difference
and talks about the time
a guy was going to shoot him at
 a local bar.
He feels he gets

into dangerous situations
in order to have someone kill him.
We make stuff from clay
representing our strength or goals
Dan makes a heart and brain.
Art has a goal of building a cabin
in the woods.
David makes little clay figures
representing his wife and kids.
Dave makes a broken family
I make the symbols
for truth and justice.
Mike had to go sign some papers
because he might be evicted
from his home.
The group clay project
results in a ball, bat, glove
and home plate.
Art makes a clay grenade.
Dave a shell and knife.
I make an archway
with a figure of a man
looking to get into the game
or home.
Who the hell knows

what it means?

Wednesday:

I arrive late
it makes me mad.
Art didn't show today.
He doesn't feel the program
will change anything in his life.
I agree.
After the program,
we will be back
into the same old shit.
Kay Ryan has a discussion
about boundaries and beliefs.
Most of the other guys list stuff
like love, family and religion.
I have nothing.
No concrete belief system
that I can identify.
She talks about family
and relationships.

I can't relate to the others.
I have cut myself off
from everybody in my family.
I feel lonely and sad
about being so cut off
from other people.
The central issue
bothering all of us.
The fear that keeps us
from functioning in society
like we functioned during the war--
Why can't we perform
like we did over there
in everyday life?
How do we overcome
that fear which is always there
inhibiting us from doing anything
with our lives.
There will be no answers
today.
Dr. Russell keeps repeating the theme.
Why in a place
where you would expect a person
to lose control did you function
and then in the relative safety

of normal everyday life
we just can't seem
to get with the flow of things.
We have to work on the issue of fear.
We draw pictures.
One of a depressing thought
one positive dream.
Dan draws a guy
trapped on an island
reaching for a ladder
from the sky(hope),
and draws an apple tree
for a positive dream.
David draws snow as depressing
and a beach scene as a positive.
Dave draws a pit and a pendulum
and a farm for his positive dream.
Mike draws a forest at night
and a college degree as a goal.
I draw a guy sitting on the dock of the bay
to represent loneliness
and a picture of an award
for some type of recognition.
I feel so out of place.

Thursday:

Do we trust people?
Why don't we trust people?
Do we have friends?
Do we feel we are evil
or killers
because of our wartime experiences?
How do we see ourselves?
Art says he takes the war stuff home
and it's increased his depression.
David adds he use to do that
but now is able to leave
the war stuff outside the home
except during certain moods.
Mike still gets nervous
and paranoid when people
visit or if he gets a phone call.
He is afraid to answer the phone
or go get the mail from his front porch.
He tells us he now has a small home improvement job.
He's glad but says he doesn't feel that way.
Dan and his wife meet with Dr. Russell.
He feels much better today.
He knows he's overly emotional.

I see a vocational psychologist.
He asks about my job history.
I don't know if it will go anywhere.
I have another appointment next week.
There's something strange.
 I feel good or up after seeing the guy.
I don't know why.
I have to suppress the feeling
as I walk back to Hell House.

Friday:

We draw life lines
from age five to age 20
or until we went to war
and then outline the significant events
of those years both good and bad.
David and Dan had rough childhoods.
Their parents died
or they were abandoned.
Dave talks about farm life
in North Dakota
and how hard the work was
and how he didn't know any different.
Mike had a stable boring childhood.

David, Dan and Mike all joined the service at 17.
Art was a trouble maker in school
so he joined the Army.
I tell a lie
I had a normal childhood
in small town USA.
It seems like most of us
were set up for stress producing things
to come in the war.

Week Six
Monday:

Have we ever really mourned
the losses
or do we even know how to morn?
I really feel lonely and uncomfortable.
I appear less nervous and
I need to continue to grow
after the seven week program.
I hope I can do so.
We have to make something
which indicates who we rely on
for support now and in the future.
It mainly deals with relationships.

We all feel alone.
I can't make any future decisions
neither can Art.
We just react.
I feel overwhelmed
and want to cry.

Tuesday:

Mike only remembers certain things
about the war
such as R & R and three battles,
During one battle, he was pinned down.
He tried to drag a wounded officer
to safety but couldn't.
The officer was dying
and talking about his family.
Mike couldn't do anything
and hoped the guy would die.
Mike is still puzzled.
He got a medal for the firefight
but didn't help the officer.
He still feels guilty
 about receiving the medal.
Art says he was a sucker

and has no faith in this country
or the flag.
There's nothing a person can do.
The war happened and
we have to live with it.
He talks about being a rebel as a biker,
and taking drugs and drinking.
He just wants to be left alone.
He will never have kids,
or a home, a steady job,
or the American Dream.
He doesn't really want it.
I don't either.
I think along the same line.
I died years ago
and went into isolation.
I see no future
no way out except death.
I'm pissed off
I'm in this situation.
Mike says the time since the war
could have meant something
but "it don't mean a thing."
We draw the strengths
we see in each other.

Art is seen as having mechanical abilities
and a strong sense of free spirit.
David is seen as guy with a sense of humor
and a strong heart but very confused.
Dave is analytical, mechanical
and a good provider but something
is haunting him.
We see Mike as creative.
Dan as a good hearted person
with compassion for all.
I am seen as able to communicate ideas.
Art draws an army helmet on a radio
to represent me.
David is having sleep problems
and awoke pushing his wife
out of bed.
Dan is having nightmares
about the problems he has trying
to raise a young daughter.

Wednesday:

David keeps repeating the same stories
about the war and relates them to phobias
he now has about going out of the house into crowds.

He would rather stay inside.
We don't talk about war issues much today.
I read something I have written about fear
but there is no follow up discussion.
Mike is distant and leaves at noon to do some work.
We draw and paint a Christmas tree.
I leave early to talk with the vocational shrink.
I'm question by an intern about problems
I have had in recent work relationships.
I see the guy next week
I am not optimistic.

Thursday:

David and Mike aren't in group.
Survival, safety, love,
self esteem, self actualization.
We need these things.
Veterans with PTSD are stuck
in the survival and safety modes.
Self actualization is when we accept ourselves.
It is slow today with not much going on.
Lunch is long and boring
with the usual mystery meat.
Two chemical dependency counselors

talk about chemicals and PTSD.
They tell their stories about war and PTSD.
The thing that bothers me most
is their point of view.
They take pride in going to war.
We deserve more and war was right,
they say.
I can't accept their bullshit.
Art likes the CD talk.
Dave says it depresses him.
The two guys brought up things
he had forgot which triggered some memories.
The CD guys did make one good point.
We veterans don't treat each other very well.
If you weren't an airborne ranger
killing people you are made to feel guilty
for not doing your duty.
We're all in the same boat
but we never acknowledge it.
One week left of this group.
A lot of waiting.
Waiting sums up my existence.
I'm always waiting.
I'm unable to go forward
with my miserable life.

Week Seven
Monday:

Well it's here,
week seven.
David is going to the hospital
to interview for another group.
He feels good about it.
Mike is nervous as hell.
Dan is worried about money issues
but isn't totally bummed out.
We are given a review of PTSD
It will always be part of us.
We can learn to deal with it.
However, some event might trigger something
in the future and we will have to come back
for a tune up.

Thinking and feeling.
Fear and anger.
Let's hope
we don't have to come back too often.
I meet with Jean.
What will I do next?
Go to the Day Hospital program with David?
No, I don't think so.
I want to wait out the winter
and will keep in contact with Jean
once a week for awhile.
I'm scared of the future
and want to keep going forward.
Jean says people really care about me.
A tear comes to my eye.
It's hard to accept that somebody
really cares about me.
We make clay models of gifts for each other.
Dave discusses an incident during the war
while we are making our clay models.
He found a chain at home with two bullets on it.
One from a M-16, the other from an AK-47.
He had shot at an enemy soldier but his rifle jammed.
The enemy soldier was going to fire at Dave
but didn't because another guy with Dave

shot and killed the enemy.
The bullet meant for Dave
was still in the enemy soldier's rifle chamber.
He made a chain to remind himself
how close death was
and can be.

Tuesday:

We see a movie
about a war memorial.
A tear comes to my eye
I don't know why.
Perhaps it was when
I saw the mothers of dead soldiers
crying over lives thrown away
for nothing.
Mike is worries about the future
after group.
He has all these things
he wants to do
but what if everything

just remains the same.
it's tough to plan ahead
any length of time
you usually just end up
being disappointed anyway.
Mike didn't like the patriotic tone
of the movie and says
it's hard to be part
of a brotherhood of veterans.
I agree.
David is angry
over having to fight
for benefits from
the Veterans Administration
all the time.
Art says a memorial is a good thing
for veterans to remember the dead.
I don't know.
I feel we ought to accept
we lost the war
and help the living.
It seems the dead
are all finished with honor.
We honor the dead soldiers
what about all the dead civilians?

What about all the guys
who have died since the war?
There is a long period of silence.
Art and Dave say they want to be happy
how do they achieve that feeling?
We draw pictures to portray ourselves.
David seems more up the past couple of days.
He draws a Coke and Dance sign
like back in the 1960's cruising stuff.
I draw a billboard that says space for rent.
Mike draws a war scene
which says everyone suffers in war.
Dave draws the same thing as me.
Art draws a motorcycle and boat
while Dan draws a wounded man
with a medic helping him.
Mike says he will take me
to a local veterans meeting
but I have the feeling
I am invading his space
and don't feel comfortable.
I back off.
I feel sorry later
as I sit on my bunk
in Hell House.

I should have gone with Mike.
I don't know what's wrong with me.

Wednesday:

David feels good
about being in the program
it has helped him
to make the decision
to go to Day Hospital
for more treatment.
I say the program has been positive
 but maybe has only scratched the surface.
I am told the program is only the beginning.
I have to talk with more people.
Jean says veterans in isolation
seem to have the most problems adjusting.
Dave says he is happier
it seems the little things don't bother him
as much as they did before.
He's excited to get back to work
and still has hope he can keep the family together
some way or another.
Art says the program has helped him recognize
some problems.

He wishes he had stable employment
and a stable life but isn't worried about the future.
Dan says he is grateful for the program
and goes off into his flowery bullshit.
He hopes to get back to work
and keep the family together and worry less.
We draw pictures on how we feel today.
A layer of feelings compared
to what we did seven weeks ago.
The pictures this time exhibit
more hope and positive feelings.
I hope it continues.

Thursday:

It's here.
The last day of group.
Art didn't show
because he says his car won't start.
It feels incomplete without him.
We meet for a final time
and give our feedback
which is basically
that the program is a positive step.

Dr. Russell gives us feedback.
Dan should be less serious.
Mike should worry less.
Dave should learn to relax.
David should open up more to people.
He says he thought I would not make it
and would have runaway the first week
I fooled him.
The group agrees to meet on Tuesdays
I won't be able to make it
I don't want to make it.
We are served some cake and ice cream
Dr. Russell plays his guitar.
It's time for me to leave.
I shake hands with everyone
take by backpack and walk out the door.
A few hours later reality has set in.
I am back on my bunk in the same old trap.
The post program high has lasted a whole two hours.
Oh shit! Now what?

I'm sad.
I've checked into
the Veterans Home.
I don't know
what is going on yet.
It's to early to make an evaluation
of this place.
Being here really makes me
feel strange, tired and scared.

What will happen to me?
I wonder if I
will ever leave this place
on my own power
and not on the morgue cart.
I hope things work out for me.
The Home is going to be a challenge.
 I need to find something
to do in the off hours
besides eat and look out the window.
I would very much like to runaway.
I'm in a room on the second floor
of a building that was constructed
at the turn of the century.
The building is condemned
and will be torn down.
Men worry
what will happen to them.
It seems the powers to be
always have ways to keep us worrying.
The room reminds me
of one of those you would see
in some old detective movie.
A real flop house type of feeling.
Man, I bet there are lots of ghosts in this place.

I haven't been to the dining hall yet for a meal.
The folks around here are creepy.
There are guys of all ages in this place
 with all kinds of problems.
It seems like most of the fellows
are missing a few cards from the deck.
I have noticed that the W.W.II veterans
really seem to recent the younger veterans.
Hell, I wish I wasn't here, but shit,
those W.W.II guys are a pain in the ass.
They have been my whole life.
Money is a problem as always.
I need to go downtown
and apply for welfare assistance.
I will get a whole $52 a month.
The Home gets the rest of the money
for room and board.
The Home seems more concerned
about squeezing every buck it can get
out of a veteran more than it does
in the veterans care and treatment.
I'm too young to be an old soldier.
I was too young to be a soldier.
Old soldiers don't die,
they rot away

in the depths of the Veterans Home.
Worry. Worry.
I feel out of place at the Old Soldiers Home.
I wonder if I will ever get a job
and put this veteran stuff behind me.
God!
This place bores the hell out of me.
I need something constructive to do
or I will go goofy.

March:

A snow storm today.
Six inches of the stuff.
I sit in my dark room
watching the wind
whip the snow into drifts
and think everything will be okay,
if I ever get my shit together.
I don't understand how this Home works.
The place is dead on weekends.
They have all these events during the week
then when the weekend comes around
everyone just sits around and bitches.
I stay in my room and read newspapers

and listen to the radio.
The Home is right by the Mississippi River
I spend time roaming the grounds
looking out over the bluffs at the river.
When I can afford it,
I smoke a cigar.
It is my only luxury.
One of the guys told me
they found a headless body
in the river the other day.
Some devil worshipers
had robbed a grave
and hacked off the head
and dumped the corpse in the river.
Bodies popping up in the river
is the norm around here.
People use the bridge
down the road
like folks in San Francisco
use the Golden Gate.
A guy was arrested by city police
for abducting a woman
then trying to cut her legs off.
It happened in the little picnic area
next to the Home.

Welcome to the war zone by the river.

Monday:

I have to see the social worker
and get my finances straighten out.
Welfare is going to terminate me
if I don't get moving.
All the damn paper work
and bullshit you have to go through
drives a guy silly.
The people in those social service offices
treat you worse than a dog.
Now I how my Irish ancestors
must have felt about the English
during the Famine.
I thought these people
are in the welfare jobs
to help people
not punish then
for bad breaks in life.
America is a great country,
if you have the money.

I think one of my biggest stressors
is lack of money.
I think in survival mode
and can't look beyond my immediate needs.

I hate occupational therapy.
I rebel against it.
It's so Mickey Mouse.
I don't want to make a damn wallet.
I have no money to put in it.
If we are to create something,
let us create what we want
whether it's right or wrong.
I visit the vocational counselor.
He belittles my work history.
He tells me to stop dreaming
and get a steady job
at minimum wage and try
to be happy.
It's not going to work for me.
It's time just to walk away
from the VA system
and resume my living hell.
At least, I would be living the way
I want to and not the way

other people want me too.
I feel like crying but I won't.
One of these days,
I'm just going to cry like hell.

Tuesday:

It's time to go downtown
and file for financial help.
I can't face the fact
this is happening to me.
I have an appointment
to see the shrink at the Vets Home, too.
I don't know why I have to see her.
I guess it's part of the game
they play at the Home.
There are a lot of games
played at the Home.
It seems more like a prison
some days while other days
it feels like living at the funny farm.
The dining experience is the one thing
everyone looks forward to.
It's the highlight of the day.
Guys line up an hour ahead of time

just to be the first to eat.

The day I start doing that

you know I have crossed over to the other side.

Veterans love to complain about things.

It reminds them of their military days.

They love to bitch about the food.

I've eaten worse.

It's a little heavy on the meat, gravy and grease.

The taste is bland but it's so filling.

You could have the finest chefs

preparing the best meals

and these guys would find something wrong.

It's not uncommon

for someone to toss their plate of food

at the wall or floor

and mention the word shit

over and over again.

Watch out where you sit.

I made the mistake

of sitting in someone's favorite seat

and table and did I get the evil eye

from an old roly, poly, crew cut,

brain dead, veteran.

It's amazing we won W.W.II with these guys.

Wednesday:

I want to runaway.
But where would I go?
I would just keep running into myself
and that's getting old.
I just want to run but I'm out of shape.
There's to much weight on my shoulders.
To much pain in my soul.

May:

I sit by the river
rain or shine,
warm or cold.
In the warm air,
I watch the boats go by
with the tan babes.
Who are those people?
Are they real?
Do they feel sad and lonely?
Are they frustrated and angry?
Do they sit by a river
and watch as life passes them by?
It looks like I'll be in the Home forever.

How am I ever going to get out of here?
It's time to stop the PTSD treatment
and return to isolation and a safe routine.
I feel empty,
an emotional pain I can't explain.
I'm crying.
I'm confused.
What to do?
Stay and fight
or take flight
and remain out of sight.
It's difficult to stop the tears.
My life is changing
I can't do anything about it.
I'm numb.
I hope things work out.
I don't know
if I am doing
what needs to be done.
My weight is skyrocketing.
All my cholesterol has turned bad.
My blood has turned to sugar.
My butt hurts.
My ankles ache.
I just don't give a damn

about my body.
I'm getting older.
I've caught old age
from the old soldiers.
If I die in the Home,
they can plant me in the flower garden
by the river.

Tuesday:

Kenny lives down the hall from me.
He says he was a Fighting Seabee
in the war.
It looks like he wasn't wearing a helmet
while constructing stuff.
He's from the North woods.
I think he was bred by beavers.
There are 400 stories
in the Vets Home …
Kenny probably has a dozen.
He looks like one of those guys
in the movie Deliverance.
I hope he doesn't want me
to squeal like a pig.
Kenny's problem is overacting.

I doubt if group or medication
will ever fix him.
Once again, I see the vocational counselor.
I wonder how he got his job.
He tells me to settle for less.
He seems surprised
I'm a college graduate
and worked as a radio news director.
It's like I left my class and
it offends him.
I hate the guy.
He makes me boil
with his smart ass manner.
I wonder if he dislikes the fact
that I'm a PTSD veteran.
It sure feels that way.
It's strange that something like PTSD,
which is related to a war experience,
is treated by the VA people
as some type of bullshit ailment.
I want to tell the guy
 to leave me alone
and let me live in peace.
"You really don't understand sir.
I am a man.

I went to war.
I hurt.
Don't tell me
how I should act
or what I should do".
I followed the one true way before and
where the hell did it get me - group therapy.
Why am I so guilty
about applying for compensation?
"I don't deserve it."
"Pull yourself up by the bootstraps."
"Forget it."
If I received some money from Uncle Sam,
I could get out of the Home,
start living like a real person,
maybe get a damn job.
Perhaps some compensation
would send me to school.
I could learn new things.
Get a job.
I could buy a house,
live in a nice quit neighborhood
and not feel as if I'm going
to be attacked at any moment.
However, compensation is not that easy

to come by.
It's a trip that equals climbing Mount Everest,
or traveling into the deepest jungles of the Amazon.
There are strange creatures
and hazards at every turn.
You travel at your own risk
and many are swallowed by the unknown.
I have a meeting with my social worker.
He wants me to start a newsletter at the Home.
I don't want to get involved
but I agree to try.
I really don't know what I am doing
but will fake it.
I doubt if the newsletter
will get far
but it might give me something to do.

I need to try something
to get my mind right.
The group stuff
isn't going anywhere.
The Home could care less
if I need help

that didn't involve killing one's self.
I find it hard to understand
why the Home doesn't do more
to help younger veterans, like me
get out of the place
by offering some counseling
instead of just acting
as a State Warehouse
for Old Soldiers
and Veterans of Lost Causes.

It's a challenge
to maintain a healthy lifestyle
and good attitude at the Home.
We feel imprisoned
because we don't possess
what we need to make ourselves productive.
The fatality of circumstances
has brought us to a point
at which we do not always know
what we could do.
But there's something inside telling us
we can be useful.
But what can it be?
A just or unjustly ruined reputation,

poverty, fatal circumstances
and adversity makes men prisons.
I have decided to take some computer classes
at a Vo-tech college and learn to publish.
The State has some money for veterans.
I might as well take the free ride.
Maybe, this time something will go my way.

Tuesday:

I'm not sleeping very well.
I'm really restless.
I'm trying to find a part-time job
but it seems no one wants me around.
I am not interviewing very well
or perhaps people see me wearing the Home
everywhere I go.
I need some rest.

September:

Happy Birthday.
Whatever that means at this point
in my miserable life.
I don't want to go to school.
I hate waiting for the bus downtown.
I hate this damn city.
I went to the nurses station
for my monthly vital sign check.
Everyone seems to know it's my birthday.
It feels very embarrassing.
I tell myself "it don't mean nothing."
It's tough getting to sleep.
I wake up every hour on the hour.
I have a few sleeping pills left
 but will save those for the long weekend.
The meaningless of this birthday

reinforces the meaningless existence
that is my life.
I am angry with almost everything.

Friday:

Almost over slept.
I can't get to sleep
or maybe it's post birthday syndrome.
It's raining.
A thunderstorm
I have to catch the bus to school.
The hell with it.
I'll stay in again today.
 I receive a birthday card from my aunt.
Why does she care?
I never hear anything from the family,
if it really matters anymore.

Saturday:

I walk over to the gas station
for the newspapers.
The whole time I am thinking
about all the sickness and death
around me at the Home everyday.
Panic Attack!
I have to get away.
I don't know.
What the hell am I doing.
SET ME FREE!
I calm down
and walk farther
to the bookstore
to kill some time
and buy a birthday present magazine.
I meet one of the guys
from the Home on the way back.
Les is moving out of the Home next week
to some sleazy motel
until he can get into public housing.
He is being pressured
by the administration
to pay back rent at the Home
because of a recent disability award.
How do they expect people

to move on
if they are always impoverished.
There is no help
to get people moving,
only the fear of not paying
big brother
 or you will be punished.
I'm still thinking about death
as I eat lunch.
Les's problem has helped trigger
the feeling of helplessness.
I wish I could lash out some way.
There's no one to discuss this with
and I don't know if it would change anything.
It's time to crawl back
into my room and hide out
for the rest of the day.
My favorite TV show is on.
 KUNG FU.
Good afternoon grasshopper.
I'm but a simple man
and must not have any ambitions.
It's time to leave now grasshopper.
When will it be my time?
After supper, I sit by the river.

It's tranquil.
I can just sit here
let my mind float freely.
No intrusive thoughts.
I just space out.

Sunday:

The sleeping pills really knocked me out.
There's a lot of load airport noise today.
I walk over to the store for the Sunday papers.
It's the beginning of pro football season.
I watch as the Vikings blow the game in the last seconds.
For some reason, that makes me happy.
A lot of angry men at dinner.
This place creates such negative feelings and reactions
or am I actually in an insane asylum.
The thing that comes to mind is Charlton Heston
in The Plant of The Apes.
 "It's a mad house…a bloody madhouse!"

Monday:

I got a birthday card from my father.
I'm overwhelmed and want to cry.
but fight back the tears and numb myself.
I'm angry at myself and feel guilty.
Why am I such an asshole
with this relationship stuff?
 Why am I making such a big thing out of this?
I just want to go and live in peace.
It will be tough sleeping tonight.
Why do I have so much alienation
towards my family?
I have trouble organizing myself
for school and feel
I am going to get lost in the shuffle.
I try hard to concentrate and focus
on the school work but it's anxiety producing.
What am I doing in school?
I use to be somebody.
It's kind of weird spending most of the day
with people who are young and energized
and noisy and then going back to a living situation
of men who are old, dying, sick, depressed
and demoralized.

Ralph, the old guy
who lives on the first floor
and always talks to me,
had a stroke this morning.
I'm sad.
It really bothers me being around this stuff.
I feel sorry but what can I do.
Don't the people who take care of me
understand how this stuff causes me
so much inner turmoil.

Saturday:

I just want to sleep the day away.
There's a memo on the bulletin board
about a memorial service next week
for six residents of the Home
who have died last week.
It reminds me of a memorial service
during the war.
We were forced to attend the service.
The empty boots lined up with helmets.
I don't remember what was said

but I didn't want to be there.

It was all bullshit.

What are they going to bury me in?

I don't have a suit.

Maybe they will burn me.

I am slowly killing myself

by not taking care of my needs.

I'm such a waste of space.

I hate the system.

I hate the Home

I hate the stress clinic.

I hate myself for being a failure at life.

Why do the dead get more respect

than the living survivors of war.

When you are dead you are dead.

I wonder why I don't give up.

Monday:

Why do I go to school?

I hate the bus ride

but it's a chance to get away
from the Home.
I'm tired of everything.
I feel so isolated
and wonder if someday
I will ever get my shit together.

Thursday:

I'm upsetting
and making myself tense today.
It's a feeling of injustice
for being taken for granted.
It's an upsetting mood
I'm very restless.
I feel people
don't take my emotional problems
very seriously.
They treat me
like I have a 24 hour virus.
Everything is going to be okay tomorrow
 but it has been years.
I have tried to be a good trooper
and do what's expected
but I guess since I'm not putting

my fists through windows
or making attempts to kill myself
or have problems with the police.
I'm not much of a treatment concern.
I'm dwelling to much on this shit
but it's the driving force today
with the injustice and unfairness.
I'm failing at trying to meet peoples expectations.
I'm fed up so I feed my anger
and overeat and stuff myself to ease the pain.

Saturday:

I expect a bus pass in the mail today.
But there is no mail being issued today
because the mail isn't issued on Saturday
at this place.
The mailman delivers
but no one wants to hand it out.
I'm upset, confused, and mad

with being screwed over
because this stupid place
won't hand out mail on the weekend.
Another guy got his bus pass Friday.
It bugs me I didn't get mine.
It's more than likely sitting in the mail
which is sitting in the office.
I don't know why this is pissing me off so much.
God, I have to get out of here.
If I had any guts,
I would just walk away and vanish.
I take another sleeping pill
because I'm so ticked off and preoccupied
with the bus pass thing.

Monday:

I'm not going to school
because I haven't received my mail
with the bus pass.
I feel like planning my demise.
I hate my way of life.
Hopelessness

seems to be a
very strong factor
the last few days.
I feel so restless
turmoil inside my aching head.
I don't think people understand
how handicapped this stuff
can make a guy.

Wednesday:

The talk around the home
is about demolishing the building
I live in.
What will become of me?
I start running the gamete of worry concerns.
I won't survive.
I'll die.
It's a great way to kill time.
I don't know
if I can complete my school assignments.
I should just hide in my room forever.

Not so long ago,
there existed in the basement of my building
a canteen which housed a beer dispenser.
For 60 cents
it would dispense a can of cold 3.2 beer

for an old soldier's enjoyment and pleasure.
I thought this rather odd
for a place full of drunks
but apparently the feeling was
that the guys would have to drink
a shit load of the stuff
to get a buzz on and before that
there bladders would likely give out.
A couple of months ago
the manager of the canteen
ordered a four month stock of beer
without the knowledge
plans were underway
to remodel the dining room.
A space was needed to wash dishes
during the remodeling
therefore the canteen was selected
to house the dishwashing machine.
The canteen would only be shut down
for a short time
so the 249 cases if beer were placed
into a temporary storage area.
But at the Vet's Home nothing is simple.
As the remodeling progressed
the administration decided

no more beer would be sold
on the Home's grounds
when the dishwashing machine
was moved from the canteen.
The room would be locked
and never used again.
However, the problem
of getting rid of the 249 cases of beer
had been overlooked
so the administrators met again.
One suggestion was to sell
or donate the beet to a VFW.
A great idea but no deal.
The VFW didn't want to get involved
with canned beer.
the season for beer events was over.
The next idea from the Masters of The Home
was to sell it back to the distributor.
No deal.
The beer's four to six month self life had expired.
The next idea was to give the canteen manager
the approval to get rid of the beer
the best way possible.
A sanitation company was contacted
 and asked if it could take the beer away.

The sanitation company considered the beer
a hazardous waste and wouldn't touch it.
The city was concerned
about the sewage being contaminated.
Finally, a man living at a small town dump
in the north woods said
he would take the beer
for the value of the empty cans.
The administration decided
after months of meetings
to turn the canteen into a fitness clinic.
I can just see all the old soldiers
spinning drunkenly in their graves.
They fought for the freedom
to drink themselves to death
now an old soldier would have to go
off the grounds of the Home
to get a 3.2 buzz.
Peace is hell.

October:

Disability compensation is a bad subject

to bring up with the folks in the VA system.
Apparently, getting money from the government,
is so bad that a person seeking compensation
is a scab on the butt of the community.
I applied for Social Security benefits
when I entered the Home
because the admissions agreement indicated
a person should apply for any benefits
they might be eligible for in the future.
I was just doing what they wanted me to do.
Why treat me like pond scum.
I wouldn't have applied
but my social worker pushed me
to file the papers and go for it.
My counselors at the PTSD program
are rather cool on the idea of compensation.
There's pressure on them
not to talk compensation with patients.
Apparently helping people
to get some financial stability
while working towards healing
just doesn't make sense
to the people who run the VA.
If a guy had a few bucks to do some things,
he might be able to get a job,

move out of the dumpy Vets Home
and get on with his life.
The big concern seems to be veterans
are trying to get something for nothing.
That's right.
I had this all planned in high school.
I went to my guidance counselor
and said I was going to join the Army
go off to some dumb ass war
then come home and get rejected
from every job I try to get
then get drunk everyday
go into a deep depression
then go to the VA and get my benefits
so I can live happily ever after.
Yes, that was the plan all along.

November:

To: Veterans Home Board
From: Resident # 32167
Dear Board:
Recently, I was awarded a Social Security Claim.
Because it was filed a few months ago,
I was awarded a back payment of $14,000.
Now being poor my whole life,
a sum of money such as this
had a major impact on me.
I thought I had some money to do things.
I began to imagine
what I could buy
or where I could travel
with this much cash.
However, I was also aware
that because of an agreement
I signed when I entered the Home
I did owe for my board and care.
At the time one enters a facility
such as the Home,
a person is usually under such distress
that they would sign anything
just to have a safe haven.
But that is no excuse.
So for several days the decision

of what to do with the money
was the dominate theme in my life.
Should I take the money and run?
Should I be responsible and pay my debt?
Or should I just throw the check in the river?
Taking the money and running
would seem easy to do
but I didn't have any place to run.
As I have done most of my life,
I decided to play by the rules
and pay what I owe to the Home
which is around $11,000.
Then continue to live at the Home
go to school and try to become a regular citizen
and re-enter the real world.
It's hard to feel good about the decision.
A few years ago a survey was taken
which asked people
if veterans were suckers for going to war.
Most people answered yes.
Today, I have the same feeling.
I feel like a chump for following the rules.
It is hard when you see what has happened to the Home
in the short time I have stayed here.
We have a board of directors

which seems more interested in the bottom line
than in people.
Dorm residents have declined in population.
The closing of buildings.
I play by the rules.
I go to treatment sessions at the VA.
I volunteer at the hospital
helping other veterans.
I attend school
to make myself employable.
Some of that back pay
would have come in handy
to buy a computer
because I am studying the subject.
I put together a newsletter for the Home.
I hope I get my money's worth from the Home.
I hope the staff respects veterans more.
 Most of us living in the dorms feel let down.
We feel like we don't know what is going to happen next.
Our sense of security has been shaken
by the way we were moved out of a building
which was condemned by the State.
I hope the board is working on behalf of the veteran
and doesn't have some sort of hidden agenda.
Payback is hell.

Sincerely,
Tim Connelly
December:

Mr. Tim Connelly:

Dear Tim
I appreciate receiving your views on the matter.
Your honesty and making assessed payment
on the arrearages was the proper thing to do.
As you know,
others who have refused to meet this responsibility
have been issued involuntary discharge notice.
Please feel free to stop and see me any time
if you feel I could be of further help to you.
Sincerely,
Don Mills
Administrator.

Friday:

A letter today from the VA adjudication board.
"We have denied your claim
for service connected disability compensation.
We reached this decision
because your experience in the war
while certainly unpleasant
do not contain evidence
of a traumatic event
 outside the range of usual human experience."
Oh damn.
The same old crap.
What does a guy have to do?
 I thought the veteran was supposed
to get the benefit of the doubt.
I will appeal
but what hell is the use.
It seems like a lot of shit to go through.
I'm suppose to get a job
and get back to the real world.

Dear Governor.
I've lived at the Home four years
and find that things are going
the wrong way.
There aren't that many of us here
and it seems we are overlooked for care
because we have certain problems
that people seem afraid to address.
 This place is a warehouse for veterans
and all the State wants is our money.
I realize there must be rules
but who is to say the rules are just.
I gave the Home $11,000 and pay rent each month.
It's 85 percent of my income every month.
How the hell
am I ever suppose to get enough money
to get out of this place.
I'm sick and tired
of being evaluated
I'm tired of having to live with old soldiers.
I feel so out of place these days

but I don't know what else to do
because I'm convinced I can't survive
on my own at this time or maybe ever.
I have more to say but who cares.
Tim Connelly

April:

I've asked my head nurse
at the hospital in the war
to write a letter to the compensation people
She comes to the PTSD clinic
for a group of women with PTSD, mostly nurses.

To Whom It May Concern
He came to us
a caring, sensitive,
idealistic, innocent
and supremely unprepared
for providing the enormously
stressful type of patient care.
He tried his best
and never refused to work
or function
at what he was capable

of doing, but he simply
was not cut ot to be a medic.
There was no lack of intellect
nor desire...the difficulty was
of a too great a sensitivity
to the pain and suffering of patients.
To demand that he function
in the capacity of a medic
was inappropriate,
there were an infinite number
of other places that would have been
grateful for his abilities.
He became a victim of a system
that could not tolerate
or condone individuality.
He has considered himself
a failure since that sorrowful time
those many years ago,
but the saddest part of it
is that it was needless,
as he was an intelligent,
sensitive human being
with many wonderful
and redeeming qualities.
The untold anguish

borne by him
for all these years
seems to be a common denominator
of so many of those
who served in his capacity.

Capt. P.
My doctor at the VA
also writes a letter to the Board.

To Whom It May Concern:
He remains totally disabled
by his problems and is unable
to work at any gainful employment.
His PTSD continues to bother him
with frequent intrusive thoughts,
dreams and nightmares about his war experience.
He is reminded of his war experience
by a number of events in everyday life
causing him to live in fear and makes it difficult
for him to leave his room or ride the bus.
He feels on guard all the time
and has chronic sleep problems.
He us unable to be close with others
and leads a very isolated lifestyle.

I believe he remains immobilized
and disabled by his illness.
He us unemployable at any job
because of this and is likely to remain so
for the foreseeable future.
Gary Falk, M.D.

It sounds like I'm really bad news
but those are the words which have to be used.
Just so I don't start believing it all myself
and fall into that helpless trap
like so many other guys have done.
-- I'm screwed up.
I can't have any type of life. --
It's as if their lives stop
and they become professional patients.

July:

I'm interviewed by two doctors
at the VA mental health clinic.
The purpose of the meeting
is to determine if my emotional problems

are related to my war service.
I filed my claim for PTSD a couple of years ago.
It was denied because of a difference of opinion
between the medical director at the PTSD clinic
and the observations of an examining doctor
for the VA board who did a 20 minute exam.
The whole compensation thing for PTSD
triggers a deep seeded anger that simmers in me.
There doesn't appear to be any logic in the process.
What annoys me is the idea of injustice
or maybe it's always having to make people believe you
or prove yourself worthwhile,
and I believe I am worthless
which doesn't help matters.
It always seems others can get help.
I'm always on the outside
because I don't deserve anything.

Two weeks later:
Another letter.
"We have granted your claim
for service connected disability compensation
for PTSD at 30 percent disabling.

$240 a month.
It is the opinion of the Board
that the constant exposure to veterans
who were seriously injured or killed
as a result of their combat involvement
has created psychiatric distress in this veteran
which supports his claim fro the diagnosis of PTSD, chronic."
Finally validation.
The money is secondary at this point.

When I came to the Home
I was homeless and broke.
I was thankful for the help
but now I must make a tough decision.
I will be getting compensation from the VA.
It's not much but every little bit helps.
I have fought for almost five years
to get this small consideration.
I will be getting $5,000 in back pay.
Now the home wants 95 percent of that amount.
If that is fair, I am saddened
that I ever served in the military.
Veterans have been getting the shaft
since day one so what else is new.
I'm being forced to make a decision

which I really don't want to make.
If I don't pay up,
I will always owe the money to the Home.
If I ever need to come back to the Home
the debt would have to be paid or no admission.
I would rather die in some other shit hole.
It doesn't make sense to me,
I have followed the rules
now if I decide not to give the money
to the Home, I am the bad guy.
This place has no plans
to help a veteran in my status
to make a transition
out into the community.
It's so damn frustrating living
in this place.
I'm not some kind of nut.
I have a college degree in journalism
and have worked as a news director,
but my life went down the tubes
and trying to crawl out
is a very slippery climb.

I have to get out of this place.
I can get into public housing.

I have talked to a couple of guys
who use to live at the Home
and have moved into public housing.
They say they feel safe.
The home wants my $5,000 back pay
from my service connection award.
I can't give the Home any more money.
If I do that, I will never get out of here.
I guess public housing would be okay
if I get into the right building.
I know it's time to leave
but even with all the shit
this place throws at a person,
it feels safe.
I don't even know
if I can function in the real world.
I'm afraid to get a public housing application.
I feel stupid and overwhelmed
about doing everyday normal things.
But, I have to leave.
I went to get my back pay check
from the Home's cashier.
I knew they would give me shit.
The guy is an asshole.
They love screwing with the residents.

I want my check
the cashier assumes I'm going to hand over
the five grand to him.
However, I just take the check and walk away.
It's my money for being mind fucked
in a damn stupid war.
The guy tells me
I wasn't in a real war
like he was and
guys like me are losers.
I want to grab the asshole
and tear his fucking head off
but I want to leave the Home
more badly and don't need any trouble.
I tell him it was too bad
he didn't get killed in his war,
then he would have been a real hero.
You can't win with the staff buttheads.
You tell people they said something
they will deny it.
You're made to look like the troublemaker.
I'm going to quit school.
The bus ride is too long.
Besides the bus I ride
got shot at the other day.

It increases my PTSD.
I feel it's not worth the anxiety.
Some days I have just stayed in bed
to avoid the whole situation.
I don't think that will go over well
in the work world.
My concentration and memory level
is hampered, I can't seem to stay motivated.
I'm trapped in limbo
I don't know what to do next.
I feel doomed to succumb in this existence
of emotional ups and downs and poverty.
I have to get out of this Home.

December:

I have an apartment!
It will be in a building
I wanted to live in.
How the hell am I going to move my stuff?
Where am I going to get stuff
to put in the apartment?
This is going to be hard.
Maybe, I don't want to leave the Home?
Yes I do!

I have a two room apartment
on the 15th floor
that overlooks the backwaters
of the Mississippi River.
It's nice and quiet.
It's good to have my own place again.
I probably can get stuff at Catholic Charities
or the Salvation Army.
I will even have to go to K-Mart and shop.
I haven't been to K-Mart for years.
I imagine it still sucks.
I was getting institutionalized without realizing it.
I feel like a stranger in my own life.

August:

I've gained too much weight.
It must have been those great meals
 of meat, potatoes and gravy at the Home.
Now, I have diabetes.
My mother died from diabetes.
I'm scared.
I have to take pills everyday.
It's not bad enough for insulin, yet.

I weight 377 pounds.
I'm suppose to exercise
but my ass is dragging.
What's the use?
I'm going to die anyway.
I will be going to the VA hospital
for a weight loss program.
It's the first time
I have ever stayed in a hospital.
I'm calmer than would be expected
from a worrisome person.
I'm assigned to a ward.
A nurse puts me in a room with four beds.
She takes my vital signs and gives me a pair of pajamas,
which do not fit and tells me to wait for the doctor.
It's 9 in the morning.
About 2 in the afternoon,
I'm still waiting for the doctor.
I haven't said a word to anyone.
I have just sat on my bed.
The nurse says I can go for a walk.
I take a short stroll around the hospital.
The doctor is waiting when I get back.
He has been on vacation
and had not been informed

I was being admitted today.
Dr. Billington asks me what I am all about.
Do I eat to please or because of hunger?
I eat a lot because of stress and depression.
He will put me on an 800 calorie diet
along with an exercise plan.
I tip the scales at 370 pounds naked.
My pills for diabetes will be stopped
 because on an 800 calorie diet
the body should burn fat for sugar.
I sign an agreement not to nap
or lay down because it doesn't burn
 calories and I will not eat or drink
off the ward. I go to the men's room
and chug a can of Dr. Pepper.
Since the pajamas don't fit I guess
I'll just sleep in the raw.
During the night a nurse wakes me
to do a test to measure my body fat,
It's a machine with some electrodes attached
to my hand and foot.

Day Two:

I weight myself. 366 pounds.

I have lost four pounds overnight.
What is an 800 calorie diet?
I soon find out.
Breakfast: One piece of dry toast.
 Scrambled egg. Four oz. of skim milk. OJ. Coffee.
Lunch: one hamburger patty, corn, plain mashed potato,
four oz. of skim milk and coffee.
Dinner: Skim milk, coffee, green beans,
a small bowl of beef stew, cole slaw and grapes.
It's going to be a long ten days.
I get trapped in the dining room
by this W.W.II officer who tells me
how an Army company is run
and other interesting tidbits
of the North African campaign.
I'm surprised that I haven't been that uptight
about staying in the hospital.
Maybe, I am hallucinating from lack of food.
I go to the fitness center.
 A fellow with a beer gut
bigger than mine puts me on a stationary bike.
It's no challenge.
I notice my flexibility needs some work.
The battle will be convincing myself
to keep the program going this time.

I wish the hospital had a pool or a gym.
I feel like doing something
other than walking and walking
and walking the hospital grounds.
I really haven't been tempted to cheat.
My blood sugars are normal.
I'm really buzzed after my walk.
I keep asking the nurse a million questions.
It must be all the damn coffee.

Day Five:

I weigh in at 359 pounds.
Dr. Billington and I talk
about how things are going.
My exercise routine will be very important
along with diet in maintaining and losing weight.
Losing weight will involve a total lifestyle change
and staying on a diet of around 1200 calories a day.
I tell the doctor that I'm tired of feeling depressed
and lifeless and it's time to make changes.

Day Ten:

I weight 355 pounds.

The news today --
a patient jumped off the hospital loading dock
and killed himself.
He was a veteran in the PTSD program.
My ideal weight may be 180
but the doctor says he would settle for 250.
Hell, I would settle for 300.
I am going to take part in a Run/Walk event
at the hospital to end my stay.
I will be walking a mile.
The doctor says I should walk
at least three miles each day.
The exercise must be doing something
to my hormones.
I made a fool of myself.
I told this woman who works at the PTSD clinic
I am infatuated with her.
I used the wrong words
I don't know a damn thing about relationships.
I'm really embarrassed.
She tells me I am a nice guy, but.
It must be all the coffee in me.
It's race time.
It takes me 22 minutes
to walk one and one-half miles

then it is all over.

I feel suddenly alone.

The whole thing seems anticlimactic.

It doesn't feel fulfilling at all.

I pack my bag and check out of the hospital.

I hope I can maintain the diet and exercise.

March:

Therapists tell a person
to get out and do different things.

Get involved with people.
It seems everything cost money.
I went to a comedy class
but the economics almost made me walk away.
I thought the cost was 40 dollars
but it was 60 dollars.
 I had 70 dollars for the class
 and home supplies.
I was caught off guard.
Now my diet will consist of day old bread
and SPAM.
I need to try this comedy stuff.
I can be funny.
I have to get my sense of humor going again.
I think from the time I was in grade school
I have wanted to make people laugh
or just be funny.
I spent a great deal of my youth
reading MAD magazine, watching TV
and listening to comedy records.
Everyday after school,
I would rush home
to watch The Three Stooges.
I would pretend I was on TV
and do comedy routines in my bedroom

for my brother and sister.
In high school,
I achieved the status of class clown.
I didn't mind the role.
It seemed to clash with the role
I was suppose to assume -
that of being a serious student
preparing to join the work force
in some meaningless blue collar job.
I wanted instead to play and have fun.
The real world seemed to serious
for the likes of me.
A couple of years after high school,
I played a big joke on everybody
and joined the Army.
It was tough being funny in the Army
since that trait ran counter to killing.
I had a terrible time grasping
the spirit of the bayonet,
which is to kill.
In war, I needed my humor to survive.
Humor, especially dark humor,
helped me cope with the pressures
of working on the wounded and dying.
The sicker the humor

the better I was at coping.
The act of being funny
or making a joke
gave me a mental break
and increased my objectivity
in the face of overwhelming stress.
In a job that required quick
and accurate decision making,
humor's distancing effect
made it easier to maintain focus
and competency.
Dark humor,
though usually revolting
when taken out of context,
also acted as a psychological defense
against frightening phenomena.
It instilled a courage to overcome fears.
By poking fun at what bothered me,
enabled me to master my environment.
The ability to joke in the face of fear
somehow is depleted in me.
I begin to restrain myself from joking
and become more high strung and burnt out.
Life has become too serious.
After the war,

I think part of the loss I was undergoing
was the ability to have fun.
My humor became more sarcastic.
I have become mired in the muck
dealing with PTSD.
To get out of the muck and mire,
I have become involved in some improv
and stand-up comedy classes.
I went to a comedy club
and came away feeling "Hey I can do that."
It has taken a while to get up the courage
and spend the money.
I'm going to an open stage
and perform three minutes of comedy.
No problem. It will be a piece of cake.
The comedy class has made me feel like
a fun loving kid again.
I have practiced twice
and have changed my material three times.
The last practice was not to good.
I didn't rehearse enough
I had a memory lapse.
I was acting like a deer in the headlights.
I have been trying to be funny and not myself.
I'll try writing some more stuff.

I went into some type of manic state.
I have become obsessed.
I am not going to screw this thing up.
I can do well
if I just focus on what I am doing.
I practice and practice and time my bits
to get to three minutes.
I am ready.
I hope.

Sunday:

I get to the club
about an hour before the show starts
to sign up for a spot.
I'm too nervous to be nervous.
I start drinking a lot of coffee.
Just what I need.
I find out there will be 18 people performing.
I am number 17.
Great, more time to have a breakdown.
I decide I need some type of cheat sheet
so I don't go blank on stage.
I write the first word of each bit
on a coffee cup, which I will use a a prop.

I am dressed in black to project my attitude.
There must be 50 people in the club.
Can I make this many people laugh?
I'm drinking more coffee and
wishing I had a cigar.
I pace and go over my act.
I'm not watching the other performers.
They distract me.
I'm in the hallway talking to the walls.
People going to the rest room
must think I'm on a pass from the nut ward.
I have to remember that a light will flash
in the back of the club
when I have 30 seconds left
so I can wrap up my bit.
I worry I might be to spaced out
to notice the light
and be carried off stage in embarrassment.
I am next.
The adrenaline is pumping.
I hope I don't go blank.
The MC begins my introduction.
"Ladies and gentlemen
direct from the seclusion room
at the VA Hospital,

The Excited Veteran, Tim Connelly."

I'm blinded by the light.

I have to ad-lib my first line.

"Are you folks having fun?

Well I am here to change that."

" I watched a special on PBS about the Great Depression.

I tuned in because I thought it was about my life.

I am so screwed up.

I got a scholarship for therapy.

I tried talk therapy but my therapist was a mime.

I went to a fat persons convention at the Elks Lodge.

That was mistake.

We ate all the Elk.

I don't have friends.

I get the infrequent callers rate

and have call not waiting on my phone.

I though about becoming a priest

but I was told I was too celibate.

So, I decided to join the Army and become a killer.

I guess that's way they made me a medic.

I probably could have gone to Canada

but I couldn't speak Canadian.

I have been thinking about writing a book about the war.

It will be called. "I Saw The Whores Of War

And Boy Were There Prices Reasonable"

I think I was sprayed by agent orange.
Every spring
I find myself chasing Chem Lawn trucks.
Thank you.
I'm Tim Connelly."
People are clapping and whistling.
It must have gone well
because all I can remember
is the flash of light
in the back of the room to end my act.
My knees are shaking like an earthquake.
I'm riding high.
I have more coffee.
Later at home my mind is all a buzz.
I can't sleep.
My mind is racing
and thinking of a million different bits
to do at next weeks open stage.
I did okay but I can't let it go to my head.
I talk with people in my class
but never get too chummy.
Some of the people who have been in class
for a long time are going to perform
for the first time next Sunday.
I will not go out after dark

besides the bus connections are bad.
I don't know my classmates that well
to ask for a ride.
I'm afraid to ask one of the women,
I think her name is Donna,
who is going to the show for a ride
because I might be misunderstood.
I work under the assumption
that women expect some type of ulterior motive.
I'm infatuated with this woman.
She is tall, with long brown hair
and so very pretty.
Who would have anything
to do
with a big, fat, ugly guy
like me?

November:

Bob, Rick, and myself
have been volunteering at the VA
for the past couple of years.
We have grown close.
A few years ago not one of us
would have even considered
ever having friends again.
Bob was in the infantry.
He was badly wounded
and still has metal popping out of his skin
now and then.
He worked for the Post Office after the war.
PTSD finally caught up to him.
Now, he's 100 percent disabled for PTSD.
He's the type of guy
who would give you the shirt off his back.
But then the next moment
he will seem so distant and cutoff.

Some days it seems like he is
an accident waiting to happen.
Rick was a scout in the Army.
After the war,
he went to work for AT&T
and became a top manager.
He had a home by the lake and
a beautiful blond wife.
He had all the trappings of success.
But PTSD along with booze and drugs got to him.
He lost everything.
He also is 100 percent disabled.
Bob has not shown up to volunteer
for the past few days.
He called me over the weekend.
It sounded as if he had been drinking.
Bob had been feeling upset
about his brother's drinking problem.
Also the volunteer program
we were involved with
might be discontinued soon.
He didn't think
he would have any place to go
to discuss issues with other veterans.
He liked helping guys with problems

related to getting benefits from the VA.
Bob told me
he had driven his new car into the ditch.
I told him
he should get in touch with his doctor at the PTSD clinic.
He said he loved me
and hung up.
I have not heard from him
since that phone conversation.

Two Days Later:

Bob has been found dead in his apartment.
He had fallen down his stairs
after a handrail gave way.
The police found empty booze bottles
by his bed.
I suppose it was an accident.
In my opinion and a few of the other veterans,
Bob had accomplished
what he had always talked about doing -
he ended his life.
I am pissed off.
I'm angry at that son of a bitch

for dying on me.
I'm not going to any funeral.
Damn the PTSD Clinic.
The staff knew Bob was having problems
but they just sat on their hands.
Bob's doctor didn't recognize
the seriousness of the situation.
I think he knows he fucked up royally.
Bob's mom says it was the "damn war"
that finally killed her son.
I haven't had a drink in five years.
I bought a case of beer
and drank myself into a stupor
so I could sleep.
I'm not going to volunteer any longer
I don't think I ever will again.

One Month Later:

It's been about a month since Bob died.
I have been staying in my apartment
watching bad TV programs and hiding in my bed
from the outside world.
I haven't been to the PTSD clinic for appointments.
I haven't been anywhere but Super America

to buy junk food.
I haven't had any more booze.
I think that was a one shot deal
to cope with Bob's death.
God, I keep thinking about Bob
lying in the grave decomposing.
Damn, that's going to happen to me.
I don't want to die!
Shit.
I don't know what to do.
I am going stir crazy.
What the hell is the use?
My therapist, Jean, calls me
but I don't want to talk.
She wants me to go to another group.
I know I must get off my butt
and get going before I am really stuck
in the depths of depression.

January:

I have started going to the YMCA downtown.
I joined a men's fitness class
in which we do a variety of exercises.

Man, I'm out of shape.
It's hell trying to diet when you are depressed.
I'm taking Prozac.
It has helped my appetite in a good way.
I'm not as hungry.
I hope I don't drop dead at the Y.
I have a meeting at the VA next week
about going into a group about grief,
I don't think it will help.
I think I will just go through some down time
then try to get involved in things again.
It's not the textbook process
on how to grieve but that's how I do it.

Tuesday:

Reality has set in once again.
Rick is dead.
He'd just purchased a cabin in the woods.
He was found dead on his commode.
The exact cause of death is not known.

But he had been drinking and using drugs
after Bob died.
He had been very close to Bob
and had been very isolative as of late.
I knew he was having a problem
with a divorce too.
Rick was going to come
to my next comedy club gig
but that will never happen.
No one I know
has ever seen my act or ever will.
They are all dead.
I thought the comic was suppose
to kill the audience.
The humor and creativity
I have been experiencing
has been sucked right out of me.
I still go to comedy improv class
it helps me express some of the things
I have stored up inside of me.
I haven't performed on stage
for about five months.
I have the usual excuses
no transportation,
or it's to dark.

I'm too old for this shit.
I have to overcome these fears
because being funny and making people laugh
leaves me with a great deal of satisfaction.
I feel like I'm contributing something
to make folks feel a little better.
That is the medic in me.
It takes a lot of energy to write and perform.
I do tend to go over board
when I get involved with some project.
I have always listened to other people
define my goals, or what I should be doing.
I have never been satisfied.
My goals have never been realistic
according to the vocational professionals.
Hell, if other people can do this comedy stuff,
I can do just as well or better.

February:

I've gone into hiding.
I didn't take part in any of the memorials for Rick.
He's a victim of the new sterile clinical atmosphere
at the PTSD clinic.
Rick really got involved in volunteer work at the clinic.

After the medical director stopped the volunteer program,
Rick felt he had no place to go each day.
Since he did not feel welcome,
he had an excuse to stay home and drink himself to death.
I know the people in charge of the PTSD clinic
will never take an ounce of responsibility for Rick's death
but their fingerprints are all over the place.
I have to do something
to keep the memories of guys like Bob and Rick alive.
I don't know what to do.
People say just forget about it
and get on with your life.

March:

Things seem to be snowballing.
Another friend and volunteer at the PTSD clinic
who was a patient at the hospital
because of a setback acted out of frustration
about the care he was receiving
and the care being given to a dying buddy.
The guy shot himself.
He went home and got a gun.
He came back to the hospital ward
and barricaded himself in his room.

I think he was going to kill himself
but the gun went off by accident and
he shot himself in the hand.
The VA police arrested him and
now he is in jail.
It didn't surprise me much.
I know more veterans who have killed
or attempted to kill themselves
over the past few years
than I think I saw as a medic in the war.
I doubt the general public heard about
the deaths of two other veterans at the hospital
who jumped to their deaths from a hospital overpass.
One guy took a dive and then the hospital put up a fence.
The other veteran just went
to the other end of the overpass without a fence
and jumped to his death.
Veterans with PTSD aren't crazed looking to kill,
but they don't like being treated like children.
Things have been smoldering at the hospital
and some of the steam has finally been released
in harmful and deadly ways.
Drastic events occur
when no one wants a serious dialogue.

April:

I have filed an appeal to increase my benefits.
One of the guys who comes to the clinic told me
to contact Senator Paul Wellstone's office.
He has helped other veterans get increases in benefits.
I guess it wouldn't hurt.

August:

I have received a letter from the Senator's office.
Dear Mr. Connelly:
We are informing you
that the VA has granted you 100 percent disability.
WOW!
What the hell.
It can't be true.
I have to call the VFW guy
 Holy Moly!
What do I do now?
Should I be happy or
should I be feeling guilty
or sad
or what?
Man, I can't believe it.
I won't believe it
until I see the paper work.
It sure will raise my income level.
I might be able to live
like some of the regular people do.
I could move out of this dive
into a deluxe apartment on the Eastside.
I could buy a new pair of shoes
maybe some new pants.
What a deal.

Do I deserve this.
I don't know.
Does Donald Trump deserve his money?
Does Pamela Anderson deserve her breasts.
I don't know?
I can't tell anyone
until I know for sure
it is true.

Thursday:

My friend Vern and I
 are going to see a girl perform
who is in my improv class.
Donna does belly dancing
and has invited members of the class
to come watch her.

I need a ride
so I ask Vern along
since he is always on the look out
for a wife.
I don't know much about Donna
except that she is pretty,
funny and smart.
I like to perform with her
at improv class.
I bought a rose at the flow shop
to give to her before the performance.
I don't know why?
I just think it's the proper thing to do.
She dances in a Mid Eastern Café
not to far from my apartment.
We get to sit on pillows on the floor
with these little tables.
I don't know what to order.
I will just have what Vern orders
which is some lamb dish.
The music starts as
Donna comes slowly dancing
down the length of the café.
She is stopping by tables
shaking her hips

rolling her stomach.
She is wonderful.
She is beautiful
in her silver costume.
She stops by our table
shakes her hips in front of me
 a couple of times.
Vern says she likes me.
Yeah sure.
A couple of Donna's friends
have joined us at the table.
Donna joins us after the dance
for a drink.
She has to perform again.
I'm at the corner of the table.
I listen to the talk and
just become part of the event.
We eat and talk and drink.
I'm getting full.
Donna dances again.
She is marvelous.
Vern wonders
if Donna would go out with him.
I tell him to ask her .
Who knows?

I know she wouldn't go out with me.
Donna joins us once again
and has something to eat.
Vern is trying to get her attention
or impress her or something.
I think it's time to leave.
The place is closing in on me.
I think I am having feelings for Donna
that I didn't really know were there.
She hugs me
thanks me for a rose I give her
as I leave.
Man, than felt good.
She smells so good too.
Vern wants Donna's phone number
I tell him I don't have it.
But I do.
I want to call Donna.
But I am so damn shy.
I have such strong feelings towards her.
I don't fucking know
what to do with these feelings.
A woman like Donna
going for a guy like me
is so impossible to imagine.

I don't think Vern likes the fact
I didn't give him her number.
Well, it's every man for himself.
Dog eat dog.

September:

I'll be getting about 25 thousand dollars
in back pay and
about two thousand dollars a month to live on.
I don't know if I can handle it.
It's warm and the living is easy.
Of course, the stress hasn't gone away.
It's still there to torment me.
Money doesn't solve those problems
of the soul and mind.
It just makes you feel
more comfortable some days.
I'm not doing much these days.
I volunteer at the State History Center.
Riding the bus is very stressful.

I miss more days than I make.
I go to the YMCA once in awhile.
My weight has been coming down
I weigh about 300 pounds.
That's 70 pounds loss in 18 months.
I never did call Donna.
She called me once
I acted like an idiot.
I told her
she could buy me a Coke sometime.
What the hell was that about anyway?
I can't talk to women.
It's more stressful than being at war.
I will buy the best pair of tennis shoes they make.
God, it feels good not to feel poor.
To eat something besides cheese whiz and spam,
real soda not that generic junk.
I can even buy good cigars
not those fake tobacco things.
Is it a sin to spend money on myself?
There is going to be a new writing class
at the PTSD clinic in a couple of weeks.
Jean says the teacher has mentioned
she might know me.
I wonder who that could be.

A woman appears in the doorway.
Tall, long brown hair, lean body,
so very pretty.
It's Donna!
What the hell?
I was just thinking about calling her.
This is crazy.
She says hi.
I shake her hand in awe.
She's with some guy.
Maybe it's her boyfriend or something.
I hope not.
I hope it's not her boyfriend
I bet a woman like Donna has a lot of men.
Good seeing you
I will see you in class she says.
Interesting.
It's a small world after all.
Maybe, I can get her to buy me that Coke
someday after all.
I don't know if I can write anything.
I haven't written much lately.
I did take part in a Veterans Art Festival.
I did my comedy routine and a poem about war.
I won two gold medals

but it's like the Special Olympics,
everyone is a winner
especially when there's no competition in your category.
I don't know why
I can't feel good about winning.
It goes back to being humble
not showing off
or having to much pride in one's self.
My family and church taught me that shit.
It sure as hell messes a person up.
Damn, you win something
but you feel so damn guilty for feeling good.
Perhaps it is survival guilt?
I can't feel good because of all those dead folks
I carry with me.
So I punish myself.
Man, this is weird shit.
I will ask Donna
if she wants to see some of my writing.
I should buy her a Coke.
I wonder if she will go?
Donna doesn't realize
we will be married someday.
I knew it the first time
I set eyes on her.

Ain't life funny.

December:

I need some time away to think about my future.
Donna and I have been seeing a lot of each other.
I know we are going to get married
I'm not sure yet how it's all going to play out.
I need to get up the nerve to ask her to marry me.
People seem surprised I'm actually seeing a woman.
Apparently, everyone thought I was gay.

January:

I have decided to take a trip to Ireland.
I will go and try and find my dead relatives.
Donna gives me a ride to the airport.
We have a preflight and farewell meal at McDonalds.
I kiss her good-by and board a 747 for Amsterdam.
My doctor has given me some pills
to relax me during the trip.
I pop a couple of pills
look out the window into the black void.

The next thing I know they are serving breakfast.
The flight is on time but we are in a holding pattern.
To much fog in Amsterdam.
I knew this would happen.
I will probably miss my connecting flight to Dublin.
The captain says we have 20 minutes of fuel.
We may have to divert to another airport.
My luck it would be Moscow.
A minute later the captain decides to land.
What the hell?
I may have missed my flight to Dublin.
I need to go to the restroom.
I am doing my business
when I hear my name being called
over the public address system.
What a strange and exciting experience.
You are taking a whiz in another country
and you hear someone
trying to say your name with an accent.
Who knew I was here?
I'm told to report to some gate
on the other side of the airport.
It's my flight to Dublin
which has been held up for me.
But my bags fail to make the flight.

Damn that happened the last time
I came to Europe in the Army.
I just knew it would happen.
It's a curse to be so psychic.
It's late afternoon
as the plane approaches the Emerald Isle.
It sure is green as the Sun hits the landscape.
It sparkles so green and bright.
I make it though customs with no problems
I don't have a damn suitcase.
I catch a cab to Dublin.
My hotel rooms have been booked in advance.
I hope.
I check in at the hotel
and go directly to bed and a dead sleep.
When I wake the next morning
my bags have magically appeared in my room.
The little people must be looking out for me.
I go to breakfast and order an "old Irish" meal.
It looks a like an "old American" meal
of sausage, ham, eggs toast and coffee.
There are four old English dames at the next table.
It's like listening to Masterpiece Theater.
The hotel is on O'Connell Street.
I talk a walk to rid myself of jet lag

and the "old Irish" breakfast.
People are selling cigarettes on the street,
as others hustle up and down the avenue.
There are a lot of cars, buses and trucks.
It's overcast.
I'm the only person wearing a baseball cap and sunglasses.
I see a horse drawn cart going down a side street.
I sit by a statue and take in the street life.
The city is full of life.
I think finding the dead relatives
is going to be a difficult job,
more than I had imagined.
 It was a good excuse to take a trip.
I wonder what Donna is doing today.
I find the National Library.
I have no idea
what I should be looking for
or where I should be looking for it.
I ask a librarian a couple of simple how to questions
about researching family history.
I discover librarians are the same
all over the world.
It doesn't make a difference
which country you are in
they are all a pain in the ass.

To hell with the library.
I will go over to the Genealogical Office of Ireland.
Another waste of time.
The information they have
is in every book about family history.
To hell with genealogy.
As I return to the hotel,
a young girl, who is panhandling,
begins to follow me.
She keeps hounding me for money.
I give her a couple of pounds
but that's not enough.
She keeps harassing me for more money
to feed her poor starving family.
I go into a shop and loose her in a crowd.
I am getting out of Dublin.
The next morning I check out of the hotel
and catch the train to Athlone.
I have no idea what I am doing.
I am following the crowd,
dragging my bags.
I make it to the train
and have a 45 minute wait
before it leaves the station.
The only person waiting in my railroad car

is a little old nun.
She is going to a Pioneer meeting
which is a temperance society
started in the 19th century.
The nun talks me out of my newspaper
in exchange for a stale candy bar.
She asks me where I am from in America.
I tell her St. Paul, Minnesota.
Never heard of it she replies.
She will pray for me,
and goes back to reading my paper.
The train pulls out of the station on time.
The scenery looks a lot like back home.
It sure is great to see green this time of year.
The train is crowded with students
and folks headed to the coast for the weekend.
In Athlone, I check into a hotel by a big lake.
The town is in Roscommon County.
 I have returned the atoms back to their place of origin.
My hotel room is very nice.
Donna was right.
There are no washcloths in Ireland.
St. Patrick must have driving them out with the snakes.

Tuesday:

I take a taxi to the town of Roscommon.
It only costs about 20 bucks.
I check into O'Gara's Royal Hotel.
I take a stroll around the town.
People say hello to me and then excuse themselves.
That's rather strange.
As I walk by a local bank,
a midget sized man calls me over
and asks me if I can help him
work the ATM machine.
I don't know how old the little gentleman is
but he is the spitting image
of my dead grandfather in miniature.
Perhaps he is a leprechaun giving me a greeting
or maybe he's just playing with my mind.
I feel overwhelmed.
It is a strange feeling.
I feel like I am home.

Perhaps my soul is here.

This is were it came

when it left me during the war.

I still recall the dream.

I think it was a dream.

During the war, one late night,

my grandfather came to visit me.

He took my soul for safekeeping.

My mission in Ireland is to retrieve my soul

and get on with my life.

My great, great grandfather Johnny

must of known something when he left this place.

The Irish don't seem all that grand.

If I had been born here,

I likely would have left too.

I have been to the courthouse and library.

There are no records of my relatives.

The trip has been a waste of time in that sense.

It's tea time.

I go to the hotel bar and order a diet Coke.

The bartender starts talking my ear off.

He has lived in the USA.

I tell him about myself.

The war and PTSD.

He tells me

I should go see a holy woman
who lives in town.
She could lay the glove of St. Padre Pio on me
and ease my pain.
He gives me a Catholic medal.
The bartender is Chris
he is the son of the hotel's owner.
He wants to take me to see the holy woman.
Oh, I don't know about this shit.
I have to be in Galway tomorrow.
The local radio station is next to the hotel.
I stop in to say hello
and find myself on live radio
for about five minutes talking about my trip to Ireland
and how I am looking for dead relatives.
One man by the name of John Conlon calls in.
He lives in Carrick on Shannon.
He says a lot of the old head stones have the Connelly name.
He says the names were originally Connellan
but the English made people change their names to Connelly.
The holy woman with the saints glove is sick.
Thank God.
Chris says he will give me a ride to Galway
maybe another holy woman he knows in Galway
would bless me.

Great.

Wednesday:

Chris blesses himself
as we pass churches and graveyards
on the hour long drive to Galway.
My dead friend
Bob use to do the same thing
when we were driving around.
Strange.
We drive down narrow country roads.
Chris tells me about his broken love affairs.
He won't let a woman use him again.
In Galway, we stop at a pub
Chris makes a phone call to the holy woman.
Just my luck she is busy.
Chris has to get back to work.
He shows me my hotel.

We exchange addresses and phone numbers.
We will never be in contact again.
It was nice to run into a decent person.
I check into the hotel
and decide to call Donna.
It costs 60 bucks
it's worth it to hear her voice.
I miss her so much.
It is time to ask her to be my wife.
Am I ready?
I have a couple of days to kill
before going back to Dublin
and the flight home.
The city is on a bay.
It's cold
the winds are strong
off the sea,
not as bad as the wind chill back home.
I walk the streets window shopping.
I stop into a little museum and sign the guest book.
The guide asks me where I in Ireland I am from.
I tell him Minnesota.
We talk about family roots.
He says my name in Gaelic is Tadg Conghaile.
I guess that's about as close

as I am going to get to any dead relatives.
The trip has been a genealogy bust.
The streets are so damn small.
I keep looking the wrong way for cars.
I feel down.
I miss Donna.
I want to buy her a ring.
I find a claddagh ring with her birth stone.
It may say what I feel in my heart.
 I hope it's the right size.

Saturday:

I'm looking forward to going home.
I guess that I have had some fun.
I catch a train to Dublin.
About half way to Dublin,
It starts to snow.
Great, four inches of the crap.
I can't escape the Minnesota horror.
The snow has found me.
My flight will leave on time despite the snow.
There is a heavy snow warning for Minneapolis
I know someone who will warm me up.
Yes

I am going to ask Donna to be my wife.
I have found my soul in Ireland.
The dead relatives were holding it
for safekeeping.

May:

It was like nothing I could have imagined.
You look so loving, your eyes bright,
hair shining, hair glowing.
Your soft skin makes me hard
as we hold each other in an embrace
of unconditional love.
Often I had dreamed of how
I would make love to you.
Each move mapped out and timed.
So new to the game and yet
our first engagement of love
seemed so familiar.

We thought we wouldn't know what to do.
Our fears turned to giggles and smiles
as we stroked each other.
I long for your touch each day.
Time stands still when we wake and cuddle.
I massage your body and feel your beauty.
Why do I love you?
Because you are so sweet my darling.
I love you.
I never imagined that some day
I would wake to the naked body
of a beautiful woman each morning.
"Oh, dear you just say that because you love me.
What would I do with out you?"
"You would be very cold my dear, I say.

The phone rang.
My wife answered.
It was Earl.
Frank Johnson was dead.
He had shot himself.
I never thought Frank would kill himself.
It seemed every time Earl called
it was bad news about another dead vet
When would the VA realize
what they had done to their patients?
I felt numb about the whole thing.
It seemed everyone I use knew

at the stress clinic was dead or dying.
It had gotten to the point
where I knew more guys
who had died after the war
than during the war
and I had been a medic.
Peace was hell.
Not everyone had killed themselves.
George died from AIDS.
Ron from throat cancer,
Pat from liver failure,
Larry from lung cancer,
Bob fell down the stairs
and broke his neck,
Mike choked on his own vomit,
Max overdosed on booze,
Phil died after too much medication
and somebody else died from hepatitis
and yeah Joe died from prostrate cancer
and Rich had a heart attack
plus...they all had PTSD.
"The Messenger of Death." called again
a few weeks later.
God who was dead know.
Earl said Rich had killed himself.

I had just talked to Rich not long ago.
Rich was talking about moving to Hawaii
to live with one of his kids.
Rich had been down
since his group leader had retired.
The group had been disbanded
and nothing had been offered in its place.
He had felt abandoned and pissed off.
Rich was found by police dead in his car
parked inside his closed garage.
Couldn't anyone understand the changes
at that damn stress clinic had caused
a storm of emotional chaos.
There seemed nothing veterans could do.
The VA didn't listen to us
or care about our opinions.

There was a memorial for Frank at the VA Chapel.
I wasn't going to go
but found myself standing outside the chapel.
Inside were a few veterans
and some staff members from the Stress Clinic.
I could feel the anger swelling up inside.
The chaplain motioned for me to come in
and join the service.

I debated but went in anyway.
I sat in the corner and listened
as people said nice things about Frank
and wondered why people didn't tell Frank
those things while he was alive.
I wondered if the Stress Clinic staff
really knew what had been going on in Frank's life
or had they just heard what they had wanted
so as to maintain their professional boundaries.
I couldn't take it anymore
and stood up and shouted
I was angry Frank was dead
and that the system
which was suppose to help
had let Frank down.
Just like it had let down Rich
and many others.
Damn it Frank and Rich were dead because
they were made to feel people didn't care about them
or their problems any longer.
A place where they had felt safe
and could come and share their feelings
and get some help was destroyed.
In the name of what?
Who the hell knew or cared.

I walked out,
and went to see my doctor
but didn't tell her what had happened.
I said things were okay
and got some more Prozac.
It was easier that way.
The doctor would likely defend the system
or make me feel I was suffering
from some sort of distorted thinking
that needed to be reframed.
It was easier
just to get in
 and get out
 and go home .
Some type of therapy
I thought to myself
as I drove along the back streets
of the city
to my little home
in the suburb.

Veterans felt recent changes at the Stress Clinic
had not been in their best interests.
Myself and other veterans
couldn't convince the clinic staff of that fact.

The staff always stayed on the course.
Any changes made
were in the patients best interest.
I found it strange
that people who had no idea
about how the veterans felt
or knew what worked best for them
could tell the veterans
how they were suppose to feel
and what should be working for them.
While something that had worked
was terminated with extreme prejudice.
The staff was always trying to reinvent the wheel
for the care of stress patients.
They were always looking for that elusive cure.
They had trouble accepting
the chronic nature of the disorder
more than the veterans did themselves.
The staff didn't want to admit
they would be dealing with the veterans
for the rest of their lives
like all stress patients
from all the previous wars
and all future wars.
The stress clinic veterans

wanted to be treated as a homogenous group.
It went against the staff's
sacred psychiatric guidelines.
The VA would make themselves look
as good as possible
and then throw the blame
back onto the veterans.
It was always someone else's fault.
The VA was always the responsible caring entity.
While the veteran, spouse or family member
was always mistaken or presumed to be troublemakers.
I was angry enough to write letters
but by the end of the day
my desire to speak out
had been squashed by a stack of letters
from the VA I had received over the years
which were full of bueurcratic bullshit and doubletalk.
I was feeling that old familiar
"it don't mean nothin."
The veterans were all going to die anyway
so who cared.
I had come to the Stress Clinic
in the ten years ago.
It was the last act of a desperate man.
Nothing in the private sector

had been of any help.
I had gotten about as low
as any person could get.
The stress clinic had accepted me
and understood what I was talking about.
The clinic didn't have that strict authoritarian feeling
so many other similar places displayed to patients.
A veteran could feel relaxed and safe.
It was set apart from the main hospital
so a guy didn't have to put up with a lot of crap
which was important in the treatment
of the stress veteran.
The safe atmosphere had been torpetored
with the advent of a new head of Psych.
Veterans blamed the new director
for most of what was wrong with the stress clinic.
The man was a poster boy
for the complete bureaucratic asshole.
Under the new director's regime
support groups
which had been in place for years
were eliminated
along with changes in the clinic's family like atmosphere.
The place had become sterile, cold and impersonal.
It was just like visiting the morgue.

It must have been hard to work for the VA
if a person had compassion.
I imagined workers were in fear
of their jobs and careers
if they rocked the boat.
After receiving awards,
the former clinic director
was relieved of duty.
The director had started the program
and had been treating stress veterans
for more than 20 years.
He was an authority in the field of stress treatment
but for some unknown reason
his program was a threat
to the established mental health routine of the VA.
Apparently treating patients like human beings
and not just as clients or patients was against the VA rules.
The funny thing was the former director got results,
better results than what might be expected.
I was consumed by anger
over the way the Minneapolis VA hospital
had in effect re-traumatized veterans
in the stress clinic in it own unique way.
Damn the VA.
Damn War.

I hated being a veteran.
A few months later
we returned from the YMCA
when the phone rang.
my wife answered.
"Honey, its Earl!"

www.ingramcontent.com/pod-product-compliance
Lightning Source LLC
Chambersburg PA
CBHW051757040426
42446CB00007B/404